# Excel 2019
# PivotTables

## EASY EXCEL ESSENTIALS 2019 BOOK 1

## M.L. HUMPHREY

# SELECT TITLES BY M.L. HUMPHREY

## EASY EXCEL ESSENTIALS 2019

Excel 2019 PivotTables

Excel 2019 Charts

Excel 2019 Conditional Formatting

Excel 2019 The IF Functions

## EXCEL ESSENTIALS 2019

Excel 2019 Beginner

Excel 2019 Intermediate

Excel 2019 Formulas & Functions

## ACCESS ESSENTIALS

Access for Beginners

Intermediate Access

# CONTENTS

# Introduction

The *Easy Excel Essentials 2019* series of titles are for intermediate-level users who want to focus on one specific topic such as PivotTables, Charts, Conditional Formatting, or the IF Functions.

The content of each title is extracted from either *Excel 2019 Intermediate* or *Excel 2019 Formulas & Functions* which cover intermediate-level Excel topics in more detail.

These books are written using Excel 2019 and assuming that a user is working in that program. If you are using an older version of Excel, the *Easy Excel Essentials* series may be a better choice since it was written using Excel 2013 and for a more general audience of Excel users.

With that introduction, let's dive in on how to use PivotTables.

# PivotTables

Before we get started, for the record I passionately hate how they write PivotTable as one word with capital letters in the middle. But that's how they do it, so that's how we'll try to do it. (I may slip up once or twice, but I'll try to catch myself. While we're on the subject I also passionately hate how their labels and menu options in their dialogue boxes don't use title case and so you'll often see that I do.)

Alright then. Now that that's out of my system.

If you learn one intermediate-level Excel topic let it be PivotTables. I literally chose to write the first two books in the original Excel Essentials series (*Excel for Beginners* and *Intermediate Excel*) in order to teach writers how to use Excel well enough for them to use PivotTables.

That's how useful these things are: I was willing to write thousands of words about the basics of Excel just to get people to the point where we are right now where I could teach them how to use PivotTables.

## What They Do

So what are PivotTables? What do they do? Why are they so special?

A PivotTable takes rows and rows of data and lets you create a nice little summary table of that data based upon your chosen parameters.

Let me give you an example of how this can be useful.

Let's say you sell widgets, whatsits, and whatchamacallits. And every time you sell one of those items your distributor (the place you sell through) creates a line of data in an Excel worksheet that has the state where the sale occurred, the retail price, and the net amount due to you for that transaction, and you want to know what you've earned in each state so you can target advertising.

You could filter your data to see this or use subtotals even, but a far better option is to create a PivotTable of your data.

Let's do that. But first we need to cover some basic data principles.

# Basic Data Principles

The data you use to build your table needs to be in the right format.

There should be one row at the top of your data table that contains the labels for each column. (I sometimes call this the header row.)

*Everything* needs to be in that one row. You cannot have multiple rows of column labels. So if you're going to have Year and Month, you can't put Year on Row A and then months on Row B, they need to be combined.

*One* header row.

Directly below the header row you put your data with one row per entry and nothing else in the midst of that data such as subtotals or grand totals.

Ideally your header row starts in Cell A1 followed by your data starting in Cell B1 and there is nothing else in the worksheet. But you can have data that starts elsewhere as long as once it starts it's header row followed by rows of data and nothing else.

The mistake a lot of people make is that they'll list information in one row and then below that row list a subset of information.

So maybe Row 5 is the customer information and then below that in Rows 6-10 is the transaction information and then Row 11 is a row for total values for that customer.

Don't do that. That is a report. That is something that is meant to be final and no longer subject to analysis. If you're still going to work with your data, leave it as raw and untouched as you can. Once you put in subtotals or break your data up into multiple lines, you can't sort it, filter it, use PivotTables, or create charts from it.

So don't do that. At least not in your source worksheet.

(As discussed more in *Data Principles for Beginners*, you should always have one place where you store your raw data.. You can then use that information to create your summary reports and analysis, or even "fix" the data. But always have that one document that is just the information and that is not changed or touched or messed with in any way so that you can go back to it if you make a mistake.)

(This helps especially if you sort your data wrong because that can pretty much break your data and you can't fix it. Keeping your source data pure lets you go back and start over.)

Also be sure to not have any blank rows or columns in your data set and to have only one type of data (date, currency, text) per column.

Blank rows aren't a deal-breaker, but Excel will treat them as valid sources of data so you'll end up with blank entries in your PivotTables.

Blank columns will generate an error message when you try to create the PivotTable because there is no valid field name for Excel to use for that column(s).

Various types of data in one column makes it almost impossible or at least very challenging to create any sort of analysis based on that data.

Okay. If you want to learn more about setting up your data in the best possibly way, check out *Data Principles for Beginners*, but we're going to move on now and create a PivotTable with one parameter using the following data table that shows state, retail price, and net due.

| State | Retail Price | Net Due |
|-------|--------------|---------|
| AK | 1.99 | 1.39 |
| AK | 2.49 | 1.74 |
| AK | 1.99 | 1.39 |
| CA | 3.99 | 2.79 |
| CA | 2.49 | 1.74 |
| CA | 2.49 | 1.74 |
| CA | 2.49 | 1.74 |
| WA | 1.99 | 1.39 |
| WA | 3.99 | 2.79 |
| WA | 2.49 | 1.74 |
| WA | 3.99 | 2.79 |

# Building a Pivot Table

The PivotTable we want to build is going to calculate Net Due for each possible state. The initial steps for building a PivotTable are the same no matter how complex you're going to make that table.

First, highlight your data.

If it's the entire worksheet, you can just Select All by clicking in the top left corner or using Ctrl + A. If the data starts lower down in the worksheet or you just want to use a subset of your data then highlight the rows you want.

Be sure to highlight the header row as well as the data rows. This does not work if you do not have a header row. Furthermore, the header row must be next to the rows of data that you want to analyze.

Once you have your data selected, go to the Insert tab and in the Tables section on the left side choose PivotTable.

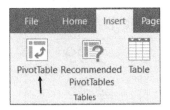

This will bring up the Create PivotTable dialogue box.

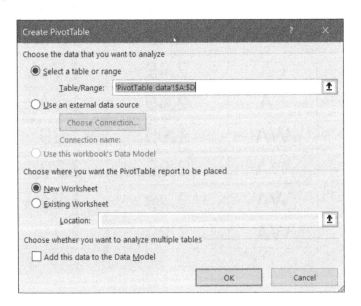

It should already have the data that you want to use selected and shown under Select a Table or Range.

(You could also link to an external data source if the data isn't in the worksheet, but I'm very hesitant to ever do this because if the external data source is moved, renamed, or unavailable that breaks the connection and you're left with a worthless worksheet until you fix that. For example, if you were working remote and couldn't access your servers, no analysis for you.)

The next section in the dialogue box has you choose where you want to put your PivotTable. I always choose to put my PivotTable into a new worksheet. If for some reason you had an existing worksheet where you wanted to put it, you could check that box and select that worksheet instead.

The checkbox for adding data to the Data Model is not something we're going to cover here so you can ignore it for now.

In summary, for a basic PivotTable you can almost always just click OK on this dialogue box without making any changes.

Once you click OK you should now see something like this:

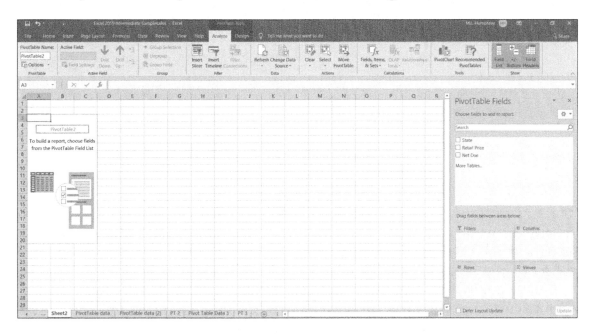

That's hard to see, so let's zoom in on the right-hand side for now.

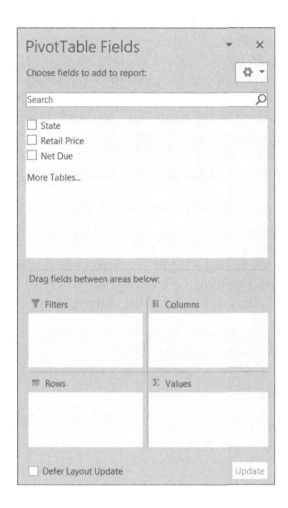

The top section shows your available columns of data which can be used to specify the parameters used in the top row or the side column of your table, or as part of the calculated values in the center of the table, or as a filter for what subset of results appears in the table.

Our example here is going to be a very simple one that will use just state and then calculate net due for each state. We'll walk through more complex examples later.

The bottom section is where you assign each field to its role. You do this by clicking on the field in the top section and dragging it into position in the bottom section.

So I'm going to drag State into my Columns section and Net Due into my Values section. (You can also right-click on a field at the top and choose from the dropdown menu where you'd like to place that particular field. So I could have right-clicked on State and chosen Add to Column Labels.

Either way, the right-hand side should now look like this:
Up top you can see that the two fields I used have been checked. (That doesn't mean you can't use them again, but it does mean that they are currently in use somewhere in the table.)

Down at the bottom you can see that State is being used in the Columns section and Net Due is in the Values section. You can also see that Net Due is being summed so that the values shown are the sum of the net due of all entries for each specific state.

This is important to check, because often Excel will bring in a supposed numeric value and default to counting it instead of summing it.

So for any field you drag to the Values section, be sure that the correct function is being performed on that data.

We'll discuss later how to change it if the right function is not being performed in the Value Field Settings section. But for now, this is the PivotTable we get:

| | A | B | C | D | E | F |
|---|---|---|---|---|---|---|
| 1 | | | | | | |
| 2 | | | | | | |
| 3 | | Column Labels | | | | |
| 4 | | AK | CA | WA | (blank) | Grand Total |
| 5 | Sum of Net Due | | 4.529 | 8.022 | 8.722 | 21.273 |

You'll see that Excel places the PivotTable a few rows down in the worksheet. (I think because of allowing room for a filter option up top, but it still doesn't really make sense to me to do so since PivotTables are meant to be dynamic and if I have more than one filter the table has to move down anyway.)

Because we had no Row parameter the table is just two lines. The first is our column labels,which are the various states listed under State in our source data.

The second is the sum of the net due values for each of those states.

That's what it looks like when we build this with State in the Columns section, but since we're dealing with only one parameter, I could have just as easily done so with State in the Rows section.

To move State to the Rows section, you just click and drag it from Columns to Rows. The PivotTable will update automatically. Now we get this:

| | A | B |
|---|---|---|
| 1 | | |
| 2 | | |
| 3 | Row Labels | Sum of Net Due |
| 4 | AK | 4.529 |
| 5 | CA | 8.022 |
| 6 | WA | 8.722 |
| 7 | (blank) | |
| 8 | Grand Total | 21.273 |

A table with two columns this time instead of two rows.

The states are now listed down the left-hand side and the sum of the net due for each of them is listed in the next column. Instead of a grand total on the right-hand side, it's now on the bottom.

Exact same results (AK 4.529, etc.) but just displayed differently.

Personally, for this limited data set I prefer this format to the first one, but if I were to add in product name on the other axis of this table then I would want my products in the rows section and my states back in the columns section.

Part of deciding where to put each field is knowing what your intent is when you build your PivotTable.

OK. So that was how to build a basic PivotTable. Select your data, insert PivotTable, drag and drop your fields where you want them, and you're done.

We'll cover more complex examples in a minute, but first let's talk about how to better format your results using the Value Field Settings option.

# Value Field Settings

Look at the numbers displayed in the PivotTables we generated previously. In both tables you can see that the values are 4.529. 8.022, 8.722, and 21.273. We know that these are currency values we're looking at, but Excel doesn't know that so it just treated them like normal numbers.

To fix this, you could just highlight the visible cells and change the formatting to Currency or Accounting using the options in the Home tab. That will work. But PivotTables are dynamic and there's no guarantee that if you updated your data and then updated your table that the formatting would hold for the new data. It would depend on how exactly you had applied the formatting.

## Change Formatting

There's a better way to change the formatting for the field you use in the Values section, and that is through the Value Field Settings.

To use this option, go to the Values section in the PivotTable Fields task pane, click on a field there (in this case Sum of Net Due) that you want to edit, and choose Value Field Settings from the dropdown menu.

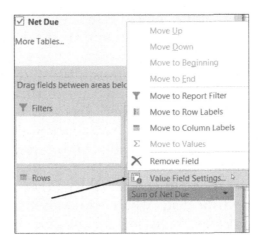

This brings up the Value Field Settings dialogue box where you can perform a number of different tasks, including changing the format of the calculated values in your PivotTable.

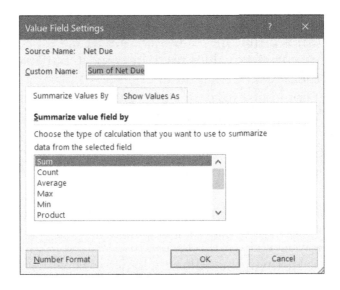

Let's do that now. First, we need to click on Number Format in the bottom left corner of the dialogue box. That will bring up the Number tab of the Format Cells dialogue box that we're all familiar with. (Or should be. It's covered in *Excel 2019 Beginner* if you're not.)

Click on the category of number format you want to use (in this case Currency), and then make any more detailed selection under that category (not applicable in this case). Click OK when you're done.

That will take you back to the Value Field Settings dialogue box where you will need to click OK one more time to close it out as well.

Your new formatting will be applied immediately. Like so:
Now all of the cells that are calculating the sum of net value have currency formatting and this will hold even if you refresh the data in the PivotTable.

| Row Labels | Sum of Net Due |
|---|---|
| AK | $4.53 |
| CA | $8.02 |
| WA | $8.72 |
| (blank) | |
| Grand Total | $21.27 |

## Change Function

In addition to changing the format of the results in the middle of your PivotTables, you can also change the type of calculation Excel is going to perform on those values.

As I mentioned before, sometimes Excel wants to count numeric values instead of sum them. Since I almost always need it to sum, I almost always need to make this adjustment in the Value Field Settings.

To change the function Excel uses on the fields in your Values section, click on the field label that you need to modify, select Value Field Settings to open the Value Field Settings dialogue box, and then select the function you want from the list in the center of the main tab.

You can see (on the opposite page) what function is currently selected and what functions are available for selection.

Sum adds the values together, Count will count how many records meet the conditions, Average will average the values that meet them, Max will return the highest value, Min will return the lowest value, and Product will take the product of all of the values that meet those conditions.

You can scroll down to see more options which include Count Numbers, StdDev, StdDevp, and Var.

## Show Values As

Before we move on, I want to point out one other thing you can do in the Value Field Settings dialogue box, and that's the options you have in the Show Values As tab on the main screen.

What we just looked at were the options you have under the Summarize Values By tab, which is the default, but right next to it is the Show Values As tab.

Click on that and you'll see a whole other set of options such as % of Grand Total, % of Column Total, % of Row Total, etc.

If you don't want to see absolute values but instead want to make relative calculations, this is where you can go to do so.

Here is the dialogue box. I've clicked on the dropdown menu that said No Calculation to show the first six options. You can use the scroll bar to see even more.

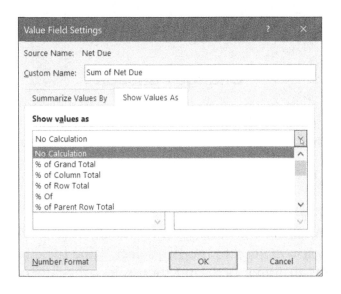

Remember how I said earlier that you can use a field more than once?

This is a perfect example of when you might want to do that. You can, for example, sum a value in one column and then right next to that place a calculation showing the percent of the total represented by that value.

Let's do that here. We'll have the sum of the net due in each state and then we'll put the % of the grand total in the column next to that.

Like so:

| Row Labels | Sum of Net Due | Sum of Net Due2 |
|---|---|---|
| AK | $4.53 | 21.29% |
| CA | $8.02 | 37.71% |
| WA | $8.72 | 41.00% |
| (blank) | | 0.00% |
| Grand Total | $21.27 | 100.00% |

Obviously the column names need amended, but we have the actual values in the first column and then the percent of whole those represent in the second column. For example, AK is $4.53 and 21% of the total.

This looks good and is easy to interpret because we're only working with one row or column label. Adding in a column label to that table would start to look messy because you'd have two columns per column label.

So how did I do this? I simply dragged Net Due to the Values section a second time and then used Value Field Settings to change the calculation for that second instance of Net Due to % of Grand Total instead of Sum.

Alright. That's what you can do with the Value Field Settings dialogue box. Now let's talk about some simple edits you can make before moving on to more complex tables.

## Refresh Your Data

If you change your original data that Excel is using to create your PivotTable, you can refresh your PivotTable so that it will show the updated results. To do this, right-click on the table and choose Refresh. Or you can click on the table and go to the Data section of the Analyze tab and choose Refresh from there.

Be careful when you refresh a PivotTable because, as I've mentioned before, they are dynamic. What this means is that the number of rows and columns in a PivotTable are not fixed. A PivotTable will shrink or grow to fit the data you give it and the parameters you set.

For example, if I changed the data table used above to include a fourth State value, my PivotTable would expand one row to show that data.

The best practice with PivotTables (in my opinion) is to work with them on a worksheet by themselves.

Do not do calculations or explanations or notes around an active PivotTable. It only takes one slip to erase your notes.

Also, say you wrote a note for AK which is currently on Row 4. But then the PivotTable updates and the AK data is now on Row 6. Your notes will not move with the data so will still be on Row 4 and now look like they apply to whatever state is on Row 4 after the data is refreshed.

This is why I often will generate a PivotTable and then click in the top left corner of my worksheet to Select All and use Paste Special-Values to paste the result back into that worksheet as data. It eliminates the PivotTable, but gives me a data table with the exact same information in it and no danger it will change.

Doing that works for me because I often use PivotTables as a one-off to summarize a large set of data. It would not work for someone who wants to refresh their analysis on a regular basis.

So, again, know why you're building your PivotTable and plan accordingly.

(There's also nothing to keep you from having an active PivotTable in one worksheet and copying and pasting special-values a version of that data to another worksheet. Just be sure if you do that to label either the tab or the first row of the second worksheet with the date you did so.

## Changing the Order of Values in Rows or Columns

If you don't like the order that your entries are in, you can right-click on an entry and use the Move option to change the display order. Here I right-clicked on CA in our table:

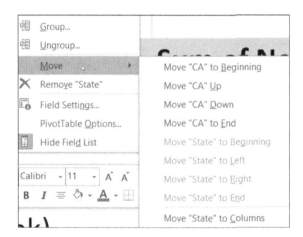

You can see that my options are to move it to the beginning of the list, to move it up, to move it down, or to move it to the end of the list.

(There's also another option at the bottom there that would move State from the Rows section to the Columns section, so that's another way to do that as well.)

If you have a lot of values and want to move them around it's a good idea to be strategic about doing so or else you'll end up moving some fields multiple times.

For example, if I move the field I want at the top to the top first and then have another field I want to move into the second-place position I'll either be stuck moving that second field up row by row (or over column by column because it works the same with columns) or I'll have to move that second row to the top and then move it down one.

I could save myself that effort by moving the second position field first.

By default your values in your row and column headers are going to be A to Z sorted but if you move things around and want to return to that state or want to sort in a different order, you can right-click on a value and choose Sort.

## Display a Subset of Results in Your PivotTable

There are a couple of ways to tell Excel that you only want to see a subset of your data.

One is to use the Filters section in PivotTable Fields to place another field that can be used as your filter.

In this example we only have Retail Price left to work with, but that's fine, let's use it to narrow down the results in our PivotTable to just those for products sold with a Retail Price of $3.99.

First step is to add Retail Price to the Filters section of the PivotTable Fields.

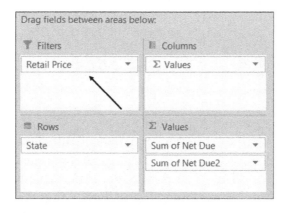

Next step is to go to the Filter dropdown menu that is now above the PivotTable and make our selection from the options there. It works just like normal Filtering in terms of checking/unchecking boxes.

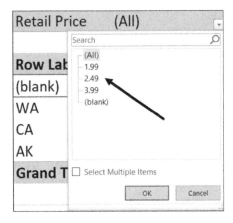

Click OK and the PivotTable will update to only show results that correspond to that filter value. Like so:

|  | A | B | C |
|---|---|---|---|
| 1 | Retail Price | 3.99 | |
| 2 | | | |
| 3 | Row Labels | Sum of Net Due | Sum of Net Due2 |
| 4 | WA | $5.59 | 66.67% |
| 5 | CA | $2.79 | 33.33% |
| 6 | Grand Total | $8.38 | 100.00% |

You can see that next to Retail Price it now says 3.99 which is our filter value. (It would say All if there were no filter in place and Multiple if there was more than one filter choice selected.)

Also, note that we don't have AK as a row in the table anymore because there were no results for a Retail Price of 3.99 and AK. The table updated dynamically to remove that row since it wouldn't have values in it.

That's how you filter a table based on a value that isn't in the table itself.

If you want to display only a subset of the results in your table using the values in the rows or columns of the table itself, you can do that by clicking on the small gray arrow next to Row Label and/or Column Label.

So here we have that option for Row Labels.

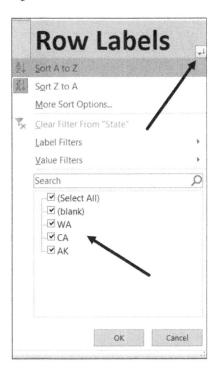

Filtering works just the same here as it would in a normal Excel worksheet. There should be checks in the boxes for the values you still want visible.

You can also filter by a set of parameters using the Label Filters or Value Filters options. If I have a long list of my titles, for example, I might filter by a word that's common to the titles I want to review like "Excel".

There's another way to hide data in a table that applies when you have more then one criteria in your row or column that we'll circle back to later.

## Remove Subtotals or Grand Totals

For now we can cover how to remove grand totals from your data as well as subtotals (which we haven't yet encountered but will when we add in a second parameter field to a row or column.)

Click on a PivotTable and at the top of the screen you will see that there is a PivotTable Tools section that appears with two tabs that aren't normally there, Analyze and Design. (They appear after the Help tab.)

To remove (or edit) Grand Totals or Subtotals, go to the Design tab.

On the far left side in the Layout section you'll see dropdowns labeled Subtotals and Grand Totals. This is where you can remove subtotals or grand totals from your table or add them if they've been removed.

You can also change the options so that subtotals or grand totals only appear for columns or for rows.

I use this because I have some data that crosses years, so it covers 2015, 2016, etc. By default Excel adds subtotals to that data at every change in year. So I'll have twelve columns of monthly results and then a 2015 subtotal column, and then twelve more columns and then a 2016 subtotal, etc.

I often want to use that data with charts, so don't want my data broken up that way. I choose Do Not Show Subtotals from the dropdown to remove them.

Same goes for Grand Totals.

As another example, one set of data I work with also involves multiple currencies. It doesn't make sense to have a grand total of currency values when that means you're adding USD to AUD to GBP.

I alluded to it above, but removing grand totals works just the same. Click on the PivotTable, go to the Design tab, click on the arrow under Grand Totals in the Layout section, and choose "Off For Rows and Columns" to remove them completely.

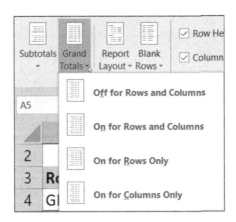

In the table on the next page, I've removed the Grand Total row from the table we've been working with. See how the data just ends and there's no final row anymore that provides the total value for each column? That was the grand total row and it's no longer there.

| Row Labels | Sum of Net Due | Sum of Net Due2 |
|---|---|---|
| (blank) | | 0.00% |
| WA | $8.72 | 41.00% |
| CA | $8.02 | 37.71% |
| AK | $4.53 | 21.29% |

Okay. While we're in the Design tab, let's cover the rest of what's there.

# Basic Formatting of a PivotTable

We'll start with PivotTable Styles.

## PivotTable Styles

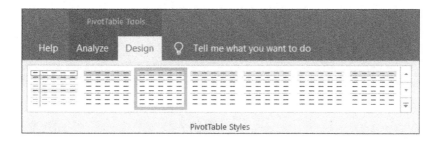

PivotTable Styles are shown on the right-hand side of the Design tab. I can see by default seven different styles. (If your screen is bigger or smaller that number may be different for you.) At the end of the visible styles there are up and down arrows that will let you see more available styles.

A quick count shows what looks like 85 different choices.

The default style that Excel uses in my version has a pale blue header row, no borders within the table, and bolded text for any summary rows.

To change that default is very easy. If you like the look of another option in the PivotTable Styles, just click on it. Holding your mouse over each style will change the table so you can see what that style will look like before actually selecting it. Here are two quick examples:

This first one just uses one color, no fill in any of the header or summary rows, and no bolding in the Grand Total row.

| Retail Price | (All) | |
|---|---|---|
| | | |
| Row Labels | Sum of Net Due | Sum of Net Due2 |
| (blank) | | 0.00% |
| WA | $8.72 | 41.00% |
| CA | $8.02 | 37.71% |
| AK | $4.53 | 21.29% |
| Grand Total | $21.27 | 100.00% |

This second one uses fill color in all of the cells, a darker fill color for the grand total and header rows, and white text in those rows.

| Retail Price | (All) | |
|---|---|---|
| | | |
| Row Labels | Sum of Net Due | Sum of Net Due2 |
| (blank) | | 0.00% |
| WA | $8.72 | 41.00% |
| CA | $8.02 | 37.71% |
| AK | $4.53 | 21.29% |
| Grand Total | $21.27 | 100.00% |

As you can see, a lot of variety to choose from and already pre-formatted to allow you to change your format within seconds.

It's also possible to use one of those PivotTable Styles and then further customize it using the formatting options in the Home tab, the mini formatting menu, or the Format Cells dialogue box.

## PivotTable Style Options

To the left of the PivotTable Styles is a group of four checkboxes that are located in the PivotTable Style Options section.

| ☑ Row Headers | ☐ Banded Rows |
|---|---|
| ☑ Column Headers | ☐ Banded Columns |
| PivotTable Style Options | |

You can click onto the Row Headers and Column Headers options to remove or add fill from the row and column headers. So in the last example if I click on Column Headers that will remove the black band from the row that contains the text "Row Labels", "Sum of Net Due", and "Sum of Net Due 2".

With a PivotTable that is using the default format, Banded Rows and Banded Columns will apply gray shading on every other row or column, depending on the choice you make. This can be very useful to have on large data tables where it's difficult to distinguish between one row or column of data and the next.

## Report Layout

Report Layout comes into play when you have a PivotTable that has multiple variables in the Rows section. It allows you to choose how your data will display within the table. We'll build this particular table later, but just to show you the different options, this is a table that has both Author Name and Title in the Rows section and is arranged so that data shows for each Author with details listed for each Title.

This is the rows layout when Show in Compact Form is selected:

| Row Labels | January |
|---|---|
| Author A | $67.46 |
| Title A | $67.46 |
| Author B | |
| Title B | |
| Author C | $148.27 |
| Title C | $90.47 |
| Title D | $46.50 |
| Title E | $11.30 |

This is the layout when Show in Outline Form is selected. Note how Title is now in its own column:

| Author Nam ⌄ | Title ⌄ | January |
|---|---|---|
| ⊟ Author A | | **$67.46** |
| | Title A | $67.46 |
| ⊟ Author B | | |
| | Title B | |
| ⊟ Author C | | **$148.27** |
| | Title C | $90.47 |
| | Title D | $46.50 |
| | Title E | $11.30 |

This is Show in Tabular Form. The first value for Title is now sharing a line with the Author Name and the summary for each of the primary variables is listed below all of the entries instead of above on the line with the Author Name.

| Author Nam ⌄ | Title ⌄ | January |
|---|---|---|
| ⊟ **Author A** | Title A | $67.46 |
| **Author A Total** | | **$67.46** |
| ⊟ **Author B** | Title B | |
| **Author B Total** | | |
| ⊟ **Author C** | Title C | $90.47 |
| | Title D | $46.50 |
| | Title E | $11.30 |
| **Author C Total** | | **$148.27** |

These formats are good for a report, but not if you want to perform further data analysis.

For that, choose to Repeat All Item Labels, turn off Subtotals and Grand Totals, and use the Tabular Form to get something like this:

| Author Nam ⌄ | Title ⌄ | January |
|---|---|---|
| ⊟ **Author A** | Title A | $67.46 |
| ⊟ **Author B** | Title B | |
| ⊟ **Author C** | Title C | $90.47 |
| **Author C** | Title D | $46.50 |
| **Author C** | Title E | $11.30 |

See how each individual row still lists the value for both Author and Name? That's what you need if you're going to take this table and use it as a data set elsewhere. (By copying and pasting with special values.)

Okay, then. Moving on.

## Blank Rows

The final item in that Design tab that we haven't discussed yet is Blank Rows. With that dropdown you can either have Excel insert blank rows between each of your items or you can have it remove blank rows that have been inserted. This only works if you have more then one variable in the Rows section like in the table we were just looking at that has both Author and Title.

## Changing Field Names

One other quick formatting option to cover and that's how you change a field name. I, for example, would not want to have a table where the second column was "Sum of Net Due 2". To change a column name, click into that cell and then type your new name into the formula bar and hit enter.

You can also double-click on the cell to open the Value Field Settings dialogue box and in the field called Custom Name you can type in the name you want to use.

(Or, if you were smarter than me, you would have done that already at the time you were creating that calculation, but I tend not to notice these things until I'm tidying up.)

# PivotTable With One Row and One Column

Now let's move on to a more complex example where we have values across both the top of the table and along the side, and the calculations in the table are for when both values apply.

I'm going to add Product and Date of Sale columns to our data. This will give us a second category to work with as well as another filtering option should we need it.

Here's the new data:

| | A | B | C | D | E |
|---|---|---|---|---|---|
| 1 | Date of Sale | Product | State | Retail Price | Net Due |
| 2 | 1/3/2020 | Item A | AK | 1.99 | 1.39 |
| 3 | 3/1/2020 | Item B | AK | 2.49 | 1.74 |
| 4 | 4/15/2020 | Item B | AK | 1.99 | 1.39 |
| 5 | 6/4/2020 | Item A | CA | 3.99 | 2.79 |
| 6 | 4/7/2020 | Item A | CA | 2.49 | 1.74 |
| 7 | 9/10/2020 | Item C | CA | 2.49 | 1.74 |
| 8 | 11/11/2020 | Item C | AZ | 2.49 | 1.74 |
| 9 | 12/3/2020 | Item A | WA | 1.99 | 1.39 |
| 10 | 4/9/2020 | Item B | WA | 3.99 | 2.79 |
| 11 | 9/3/2020 | Item B | WA | 2.49 | 1.74 |
| 12 | 2/2/2020 | Item A | WA | 3.99 | 2.79 |

And here's our new selection options pane with State in the Columns section, Product in the Rows section, Net Due in the Values section, and Date of Sale in the Filter section.

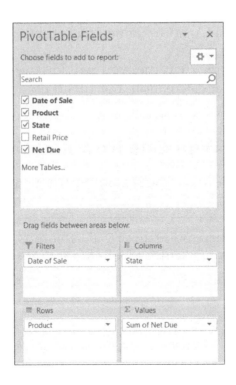

This is what that looks like in the PivotTable itself:

| | A | B | C | D | E | F | G |
|---|---|---|---|---|---|---|---|
| 1 | Date of Sale | (All) | | | | | |
| 2 | | | | | | | |
| 3 | Sum of Net Due | Column Labels | | | | | |
| 4 | Row Labels | AK | AZ | CA | WA | (blank) | Grand Total |
| 5 | Item A | | 1.393 | 4.536 | 4.186 | | 10.115 |
| 6 | Item B | | 3.136 | | 4.536 | | 7.672 |
| 7 | Item C | | | 1.743 | 1.743 | | 3.486 |
| 8 | (blank) | | | | | | |
| 9 | Grand Total | | 4.529 | 1.743 | 6.279 | 8.722 | 21.273 |

The values in the middle of the table are the sum of the Net Due for each combination of State and Product.

So Cell D5 which is 4.536 is the total net due for sales of Item A in CA. (The AK amounts are a little hard to read right now because the width of Column B is based on the text "Column Labels" and the values in the table are all right-aligned by default.)

Also, a quick note: if the PivotTable Fields task pane ever disappears on you, just click onto your PivotTable to bring it back. (If you're not actively working in the PivotTable that task pane as well as the extra PivotTable Tools tabs at the top go away.)

## Pivot Table With Multiple Criteria In Rows and Columns

Now let's move on to a third, more complex example that has multiple criteria in both the rows and columns of the table. Here are the first few rows from the data we're going to use:

| | A | B | C | E | F | G | H | I |
|---|---|---|---|---|---|---|---|---|
| 1 | Month | Year | Title | Author Name | Quantity | Royalty | Ad Cost | P or L |
| 2 | January | 2015 | Title A | Author A | 0.00 | $0.00 | | $0.00 |
| 3 | January | 2015 | Title C | Author C | 84.00 | $108.82 | | $108.82 |
| 4 | January | 2015 | Title D | Author C | 23.00 | $33.74 | | $33.74 |

And here is the first portion of the PivotTable created with that data:

| ⊿ | A | B | C | D | E | F |
|---|---|---|---|---|---|---|
| 1 | | | | | | |
| 2 | | | | | | |
| 3 | Sum of P or L | Column Labels ⌄ | | | | |
| 4 | | ⊟ 2015 | | | | |
| 5 | Row Labels ⌄ | January | February | March | April | May |
| 6 | ⊟ Author A | $0.00 | $6.23 | $11.76 | $4.80 | $6.79 |
| 7 | Title A | $0.00 | $6.23 | $11.76 | $4.80 | $6.79 |
| 8 | ⊟ Author B | | $0.52 | | | |
| 9 | Title B | | $0.52 | | | |
| 10 | ⊟ Author C | $142.56 | $59.69 | $26.81 | $10.83 | |
| 11 | Title C | $108.82 | $28.07 | $9.36 | $5.41 | |
| 12 | Title D | $33.74 | $20.37 | $9.43 | $2.71 | |
| 13 | Title E | | $11.25 | $8.02 | $2.71 | |
| 14 | ⊟ (blank) | | | | | |
| 15 | (blank) | | | | | |
| 16 | Grand Total | $142.56 | $66.44 | $38.57 | $15.63 | $6.79 |

The columns section has year and then month. The rows section has Author and then Title. It's important if you're going to use multiple parameters that you get them in the right order in the PivotFields section or else your data can get very ugly very fast.

Here is what that looks like for this table:

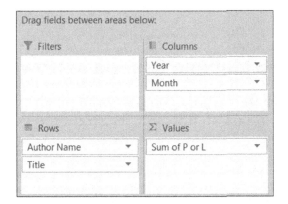

You can see that I have Year above Month and Author above Title. That sets the display order in the PivotTable so that all of the months for a specific year are listed first and then all of the months for the next year. Same with all of the titles for a specific author before the titles for the next author are listed.

If your data is displaying in the wrong order. Say, for example, I had Month above Year in that Columns section which would put all of January's results for every year first and then all of February's results for every year next, etc., it's a simple matter of clicking and dragging one of the fields into the correct order.

The table will update immediately with your changes so you can quickly see if you got it right.

One more note on this. Using multiple fields does not always work well. I almost always avoid using multiple fields in the Values section if I have more than one field in the Columns section. It just gets too busy to read easily.

## Remove a Field

Another tip that we haven't talked about yet is what to do if you've placed a field into Filters, Columns, Rows, or Values and you decide you don't want it there.

One option is to click on the field name and choose Remove Field from the dropdown menu. Another is to uncheck the box next to the field name in the choose fields section. (That only works if you want to remove all uses of the field or if it was just used a single time.) You can also right-click on the field in the table itself and choose the Remove option from the dropdown there.

## Hide Second-Level Data

Another thing you can do if you have multiple levels of data is hide the details from the second level of data so that you only see the summary values that pertain to the first level of data. You can do this on a case-by-case basis.

So in this data set we actually have data for 2015, 2016, 2017, 2018, 2019, and 2020.

2015 was not a very exciting year and it was a while ago. So maybe I don't care about seeing month-by-month data for that particular year.

I can click on the small negative sign next to 2015 and that will hide the monthly data for 2015 and just give me summary results. like so:

| Sum of P or L | Column Labels | | |
|---|---|---|---|
| | ⊞ 2015 | ⊟ 2016 | |
| Row Labels | | January | February |
| ⊟ Author A | $51.09 | $3.47 | $2.98 |
| Title A | $51.09 | $3.47 | $2.98 |
| ⊟ Author B | $1.87 | | |

Note that the minus sign is now a plus sign. To bring back the more detailed results, you just click on that + sign.

I could do the same on the left-hand side with Author so that I'm only seeing summary results at the Author level instead of the Title level.

To collapse all of the results at once instead of one-by-one, you can click into a cell in that row or column, right-click, and choose Collapse Entire Field.

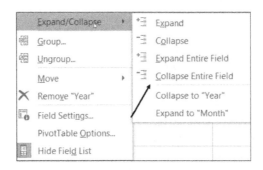

To expand it again, right-click and choose Expand Entire Field. Three's also an option to Expand or Collapse to a named level, "Year" or "Month", for example, which would come in useful if you had three levels of data in a row or column.

## Grouping and Ungrouping

Another thing you can do in a PivotTable that I use somewhat often is group different selections.

For example, I have published audiobooks through two different distributors, ACX and Authors Republic. When I pull in my sales data it comes in under those two names. But sometimes when I'm generating summary reports I just want to look at overall audiobook numbers rather than specific numbers for each of those distributors.

There's no way for Excel to know that those two belong together without my somehow telling it that I want them grouped. (I could add a column to my data that puts them in an audiobook group, but since I haven't done that...)

To group two of the values in a column or row, highlight the labels of the rows or columns you want to group.

(They do not need to be next to one another. If they aren't you can use the Ctrl key as you select each one.)

Next, right-click and selected Group from the dropdown menu or go to the PivotTable Tools Analyze tab and choose Group Selection from there.

The entries you chose to group will now be next to one another and your data will have another level to it.

The group you created will be labeled Group 1, the rest of the entries at the new level will be labeled identically to their prior name.

Like so where I have chosen to Group Author A and Author C and they are now in Group 1 but Author B was left by itself so is now in a group labeled Author B:

| Row Labels | |
|---|---|
| − Group1 | 142.56 |
| + Author A | 0 |
| + Author C | 142.56 |
| − Author B | |
| + Author B | |
| + (blank) | |
| Grand Total | 142.56 |

You can change the group name by clicking on the cell with the group name in it and then using the formula bar to type in the new name. Hit enter when you're done.

To ungroup values, click on a group name, right-click, and choose ungroup. This will remove all groupings at that level. You can also use the Ungroup option in the Analyze tab of the PivotTable Tools.

## PivotTable Tools Analyze Tab

We've covered a lot so far and that's most of what I do in PivotTables, but there is a handy dandy Analyze tab under PivotTable Tools that's at least worth a quick look. Some of it we discussed already, like Refresh and Group/Ungroup, but let's walk through a few more of your options.

I'm going to do these in order of what I use rather than in order withing the tab so that if you start to get bored reading through this section you can just skip to the next section.

## Fields, Items, & Sets

In addition to the calculations we already discussed, Excel allows you to add calculated fields to your table that combine more than one of the fields in your table to create a new value.

For example, let's say that I want to know my profit or loss per unit for my titles. I have a field that tells me units sold, Quantity, and I have a field that tells me total Profit and Loss, P or L. I can use the Calculated Field option under Fields, Items, & Sets to have Excel calculate P or L divided by Quantity for me with the data in the PivotTable.

Why do it this way instead of doing it in the source data table? Because in the source data we haven't aggregated our results. So I could calculate for every month what the profit or loss per unit was for a specific title and then take the average of those values, but I couldn't calculate the overall number since my data isn't aggregated until I do so through the PivotTable.

Let's walk through how to do that. Here's what we're going to start with. I've changed the column names, formatted the values, and filtered this to just 2015 data. (Note that when I changed the column name it also changed the name in the PivotTable Fields task pane so be aware that happens.)

| Year | 2015 | |
|---|---|---|
| **Row Labels** | **Units** | **Profit** |
| −**Author A** | **27** | **$51.09** |
| Title A | 27 | $51.09 |
| −**Author B** | **2** | **$1.87** |
| Title B | 2 | $1.87 |
| −**Author C** | **405** | **$298.73** |
| Title C | 263 | $162.84 |
| Title D | 86 | $90.14 |
| Title E | 55 | $45.75 |
| **Grand Total** | **434** | **$351.69** |

Click on the PivotTable and then go to the Analyze tab under PivotTable Tools.

In the Calculations section click on the dropdown for Fields, Items, & Sets and choose Calculated Field.

You'll then see the Inert Calculated Field dialogue box.

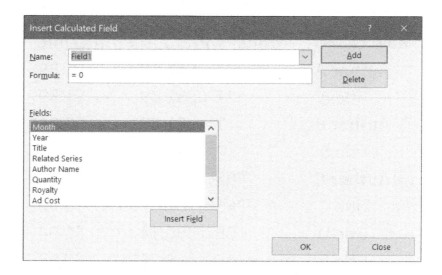

Under Name, type the name you want to use for the field.

Under Formula you need to type in a formula that will do your calculation. (We covered basic math operators in *Excel 2019 Beginner*. Use a plus sign for addition, minus sign for subtraction, asterisk for multiplication, and forward slash for division. If you want to do something more than that then look to *Excel 2019 Formulas and Functions* or use the Help function in Excel.)

You can click on the field names you need as you build your formula. They will be the original field names. So I clicked into that Formula box, left the = sign, deleted the 0, clicked on P or L, then typed a forward slash, then clicked on Quantity.

When you're done, click on Add. And then click on OK. Excel should add the new calculated field into your PivotTable. (If you don't click Add it may just add it to the list of available fields in the PivotTable Fields task pane.)

You can then format the new value like you would any other either in the PivotTable Fields task pane or the PivotTable cells themselves.

Because this was a summary table, Excel named the field in the table Sum of Profit Per Unit but what it's actually calculating is Profit divided by Units. So I'm going to ahead and rename it in my table but I have to tweak the name a bit because Excel won't let me use Profit Per Unit since that was the original name I used.

Here's what I end up with. A table that now has a third column Profit/Unit which is calculated based upon the values in two other cells in my table.

| Year | 2015 | | |
|---|---|---|---|
| **Row Labels** | **Units** | **Profit** | **Profit/Unit** |
| ⊟**Author A** | 27 | $51.09 | $1.89 |
| Title A | 27 | $51.09 | $1.89 |
| ⊟**Author B** | 2 | $1.87 | $0.94 |
| Title B | 2 | $1.87 | $0.94 |
| ⊟**Author C** | 405 | $298.73 | $0.74 |
| Title C | 263 | $162.84 | $0.62 |
| Title D | 86 | $90.14 | $1.04 |
| Title E | 55 | $45.75 | $0.83 |
| **Grand Total** | **434** | **$351.69** | **$0.81** |

The nice thing about using calculated values is they adjust as you move the table around. I could have done this same calculation off to the side of the table for one row but it would've stayed in place if/when I updated the table and may not have lined up anymore to the correct row in the table.

Which reminds me that there is an issue if you do calculations outside of a PivotTable that use values in a PivotTable: The calculations do not move with the PivotTable. The cell references the calculation uses are basically the set of rules that build that specific value in the PivotTable.

It sounds confusing. Let me show you.

If I use the values in this PivotTable to divide the value in C5 (which is $51.09) by the value in B5 (which is 27 units), the formula Excel creates looks like this:

=GETPIVOTDATA("Profit",$A$4,"Author Name","Author A")/
GETPIVOTDATA("Units",$A$4,"Author Name","Author A")

That is very different from the formula it would create if this weren't a PivotTable. If this weren't a PivotTable it would be =C5/B5.

That difference means that even as the table is updated and values move around, this calculation will continue to use the values for profit and units for Author A.

The way the calculation is structured makes it impossible to quickly create and copy a formula that references cells in a Pivot Table. You have to create the calculation one row at a time. (Or use a calculated field in the table like we just did, or do what I often do which is build the table, copy and paste special to turn it back into only values and then do the extra calculation.)

Okay. On to the next one.

## Change Data Source

Change Data Source can be found in the Data section of the Analyze tab. It allows you to change the data that is being used in your current PivotTable.

Even when I use the top left corner of a worksheet to tell Excel to Select All of my data to build a PivotTable what Excel actually does is finds the limits of my existing data and defines the data range to use that way.

So, for example, with the latest data set we were working with, Excel gave the data range as 'Pivot Table Data 3'!$A:$I.

That's saying that the data in use was coming from a worksheet named Pivot Table Data 3 and Columns A through I of that worksheet. But what happens if I add on more data into Column J? Or Column K?

Excel will not automatically pick up that new data. If I don't want to start over with a new PivotTable, I have to go in and change the data source instead.

To do so, go to the Analyze tab, click on Change Data Source and then Change Data Source again in the dropdown menu.

That will open a Change PivotTable Data Source dialogue box.

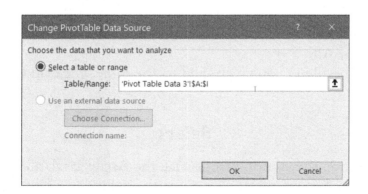

In this case, if I just wanted to change the range to include Column J, I could quickly click into that box and replace the I with a J and then click on OK. Once I did that my new field name would appear in the PivotTable Fields task pane

Another option is to use the backspace key to delete the current range, and then select your whole data range again.

Whatever you do, do not click into that space and try to use the arrow keys. If you do that, click cancel and try again. (When you use the arrow keys you're actually moving your cursor around within the data set and Excel is updating the data range to use but it's doing it one cell at a time. You could fix this by arrowing to the edge of your data set and then using the shift key as you select the rest of your data, but I find it easier to never go down that road in the first place.)

## Refresh

We already discussed that you can use the Refresh option in the Data section of the Analyze tab to update the data in your table in case a change was made in the data set that Excel was pulling from.

I'm just going to make one more point here, which is that if you generate your PivotTable and find that there's an issue, for example, customer Albert Jones was entered as Albert Jones and Albert R. Jones, it's better to update the source data for your table than to try to manually fix it within the PivotTable. Manually fixing it fixes it just that one time. Updating it in the source data fixes it for life.

(Of course, in that kind of situation I would recommend having the raw data somewhere that you never ever touch and then the working data stored somewhere that you can fix. Just document what you've done.)

## Clear

If you want to keep the PivotTable but start over fresh by removing all fields and settings, you can click on Clear in the Actions section of the Analyze tab, and then choose Clear All

To clear just the filters you've applied to the table, click on Clear and choose Clear Filters.

## Select

The Select option in the Actions section of the Analyze tab allows you to Select the entire PivotTable, just the labels, or just the values. Click on Select to see the dropdown menu of your options.

Initially your only choice will be Entire PivotTable which will highlight all of the cells in the table, including any filters.

You can then choose Labels or Values from the dropdown and it will confine your selection to just the labels in the table or the values in the table. (There is also a Labels and Values option but that appears to be the same as Entire PivotTable.)

If you had a PivotTable on a worksheet with a bunch of other information and just wanted to copy that PivotTable, this option would let you do that.

## Move PivotTable

The Move PivotTable option in the Actions section of the Analyze tab allows you to move your entire PivotTable to a new worksheet or another location in the current worksheet. This is useful when you have other data in the worksheet and want to just move the PivotTable.

(When I was playing around with all of this I couldn't insert rows because of a PivotTable in an existing worksheet and used Move PivotTable to put that table elsewhere.)

## Insert Slicer

Insert Slicer basically works like a filter except that the criteria you can choose from are visible on the screen in a separate dialogue box.

To insert a Slicer go to the Analyze tab under PivotTable Tools and choose Insert Slicer from the Filter section. That will bring up a list of your available fields, click on one and a slicer will appear on the screen that lists all of the values for that field.

| Year | 2015 | | | Title | | |
|---|---|---|---|---|---|---|
| | | | | Title A | | |
| Row Labels | Units | Profit | Profit/Unit | Title B | | |
| Author B | 2 | $1.87 | $0.94 | | | |
| Title B | 2 | $1.87 | $0.94 | Title C | | |
| Grand Total | 2 | $1.87 | $0.94 | Title D | | |
| | | | | Title E | | |
| | | | | (blank) | | |

Here I've created a Slicer for Title and then selected just Title B. You can see that the PivotTable updated to show that.

To select more than one field you can use the shift or control keys or you can click on the multi-select option at the top. It's the list with the checkmarks next to each line. After you select that, you can click on all the fields you want without needing to use Ctrl or shift. If you use multi-select, click on it again to turn it off.

To clear your selection, click on the funnel image in the top right corner of the slicer box or use Alt + C. (You may have to click on it more than once depending on where you were before you tried to click on it.)

You can also have more than one slicer open at once.

When you have a slicer open and are clicked onto it, there will be a Slicer Tools Options tab available that lets you format the slicer and determine its position on the page.

Slicers can be useful if you want to filter your data by more than one value and want to see what values you've chosen since in that case the standard Filter option would just show Multiple.

It can also come in handy if you are giving access to the PivotTable to other users and you want them to be able to click on the available choices without having to use a Filter dropdown.

To remove a slicer, click on it and then hit the delete key.

## Insert Timeline

Insert Timeline works with date fields and lets you narrow down your results by month, quarter, year, or day.

This is very handy for data where you have just the date (8/9/15) but want to see the data by month or year without having to add new fields to your original data source. (And certainly beats my old method of filtering by date and then checking/unchecking boxes.)

Here is a timeline from our second data set which included Date of Sale:

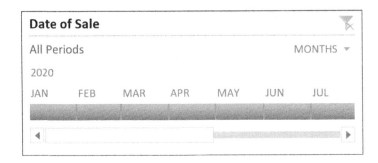

You can either click on those individual months to see the data for a specific month or that dropdown on the right can be changed to show years, quarters, or days instead.

I have at times found Excel didn't want to acknowledge a field as a valid date field, but when it does, using the timeline is very helpful.

# Conclusion

So that was PivotTables. If you want to learn more niche topics, check out the rest of the series which covers Charts, Conditional Formatting, and the IF Functions. Or if you want to now explore a broader range of topics you can choose Excel 2019 Intermediate or Excel 2019 Formulas & Functions which cover those topics and more.

# Appendix A: Basic Terminology

Most of the terminology I use is pretty standard but I think I do have a few quirks in how I refer to things, so be sure to do a quick skim of this section just to make sure we're on the same page. This is meant to be a refresher only. These terms were initially taught in *Excel 2019 Beginner*.

## Column

Excel uses columns and rows to display information. Columns run across the top of the worksheet and, unless you've done something funky with your settings, are identified using letters of the alphabet.

## Row

Rows run down the side of the worksheet and are numbered starting at 1 and up to a very high number. In Excel 2019 that number is 1048576.

## Cell

A cell is a combination of a column and row that is identified by the letter of the column it's in and the number of the row it's in. For example, Cell A1 is the cell in the first column and first row of a worksheet.

## Click

If I tell you to click on something, that means to use your mouse (or trackpad) to move the cursor on the screen over to a specific location and left-click or right-click on the option. (See the next definition for the difference between left-click and right-click).

If you left-click, this generally selects the item. If you right-click, this generally creates a dropdown list of options to choose from. If I don't tell you which to do, left- or right-click, then left-click.

## Left-click/Right-click

If you look at your mouse or your trackpad, you generally have two flat buttons to press. One is on the left side, one is on the right. If I say left-click that means to press down on the button on the left. If I say right-click that means press down on the button on the right. (If you're used to using Word or Excel you may already do this without even thinking about it. If that's the case then think of left-click as what you usually use to select text and right-click as what you use to see a menu of choices.)

# Spreadsheet

I'll try to avoid using this term, but if I do use it, I'll mean your entire Excel file. It's a little confusing because it can sometimes also be used to mean a specific worksheet, which is why I'll try to avoid it as much as possible.

# Worksheet

This is the term I'll use as much as possible. A worksheet is a combination of rows and columns that you can enter data in. When you open an Excel file, it opens to Sheet1.

# Workbook

I don't use this term often, but it may come up. A workbook is an Excel file and can contain multiple worksheets. The default file type for an Excel 2019 workbook is a .xlsx file type.

# Formula Bar

This is the long white bar at the top of the screen with the $f\chi$ symbol next to it.

# Tab

I refer to the menu choices at the top of the screen (File, Home, Insert, Page Layout, Formulas, Data, Review, View, and Help) as tabs. Note how they look like folder tabs from an old-time filing system when selected? That's why.

# Data

I use data and information interchangeably. Whatever information you put into a worksheet is your data or data set.

# Select

If I tell you to "select" cells, that means to highlight them. Same with text.

# Arrow

If I say that you can "arrow" to something that just means to use the arrow keys to navigate from one cell to another.

# Cell Notation

We may end up talking about cell ranges in this book. Excel uses a very specific type of cell notation. We already mentioned that a cell is referenced based upon the letter of its column and the number of its row. So A1 is the cell in Column A and Row 1. (When used as cell notation you don't need to include Cell before the A1.)

To reference a range of cells Excel uses the colon (:) and the comma (,). A colon between cells means "through". So A1:B25 means all of the cells between Cell A1 and Cell B25 which is all of the cells in Columns A and B and Rows 1 through 25. A comma means and. So A1,B25 would be Cells A1 and B25 only.

When in doubt, go into Excel, type = and the cell range, hit enter, and then double-click back into that cell. Excel will highlight all of the cells in the range you entered.

# Dialogue Box

I will sometimes refer to dialogue boxes. These are the boxes that occasionally pop up with additional options for you to choose from for a particular task.

# Paste Special – Values

Paste Special - Values is a special type of pasting option which I often use to remove formulas from my data or to remove a pivot table but keep the table it created. If I tell you to Paste Special - Values that means use the Values paste option which is the one with a 123 on the clipboard.

# Dropdown

I will occasionally refer to a dropdown or dropdown menu. This is generally a list of potential choices that you can select from if you right-click on your worksheet or on one of the arrows next to an option in the tabs at the top. For example, if you go to the Home tab and click on the arrow under Paste, you will see additional options listed in a paste dropdown menu.

## Task Pane

I am going to call the separate standalone pane that appears on the right-hand side of the screen on occasion a task pane. These appear for PivotTables, charts, and the Help function.

## About the Author

M.L. Humphrey is a former stockbroker with a degree in Economics from Stanford and an MBA from Wharton who has spent close to twenty years as a regulator and consultant in the financial services industry.

You can reach M.L. Humphrey at:

mlhumphreywriter@gmail.com

or at

www.mlhumphrey.com

Made in the USA
Monee, IL
04 February 2022

90607384R00031